The I Ching of Management

The I Ching of Management

An Age-Old Study for
New Age Managers

William Sadler

HUMANICS PUBLISHING GROUP
Atlanta, Georgia

HUMANICS PUBLISHING GROUP
PO Box 7400
Atlanta, Georgia 30309 USA

Humanics Publishing Group is an imprint of Humanics Limited.

First Edition

PRINTED IN THE UNITED STATES OF AMERICA

Library of Congress Cataloging-in-Publication Data

Sadler, William, 1931-
        The I Ching of Management.
        1. Organizational management. 2. I Ching. 3. Taoism.

HD37.C47M47   1996658—dc20   96-46065
ISBN 0-89334-242-4
CIP

Table of Contents

I. The I Ching

The History of the I Ching
Lao Tzu and Taoism
Confucius
Yin and Yang
The Trigrams
The Hexagrams
Generating the Hexagrams

II. Interpretation of the Hexagrams

24.	Return	Fu
25.	Fidelity	Wu Wang
26.	Nurturance of the Great	Ta Ch'u
27.	Nourishment	I
28.	Excess	Ta Kuo
29.	Pitfalls	K'an
30.	Fire	Li
31.	Sensitivity	Hsien
32.	Constancy	Heng
33.	Withdrawal	Tun
34.	Great Power	Ta Chuang
35.	Advance	Chin
36.	Concealment of Illumination	Ming I
37.	Inner Governance	Chia Jen
38.	Disharmony	K'uei
39.	Halting	Chien
40.	Liberation and Freedom	Hsieh
41.	Reduction	Sun
42.	Increase	I
43.	Parting	Kuai
44.	Meeting	Kou
45.	Gathering	Ts'ui
46.	Rising	Sheng
47.	Exhaustion	K'un
48.	The Well	Ching
49.	Riddance	Ko
50.	Refined Heating	Ting
51.	Action	Chen
52.	Stillness/Stopping	Ken
53.	Gradual Progress	Chien
54.	Intercourse is Not Proper	Kuei Mei
55.	Richness	Feng
56.	Travel	Lu
57.	Flexibility and Obedience	Sun
58.	Joy	Tui
59.	Dispersal	Huan
60.	Discipline	Chieh

I
The I Ching

I. The I Ching

The Tao Te Ching arrives in the twentieth century after more than 4,000 years as a still vibrant body of knowledge and wisdom, amply testified to by the many "new age" Tao books offered to the reading public. The teachings of the I Ching represent great practical value as a guide to the manager, because the art and skill of management go beyond being a "boss" or "leader". The needs and resources of the 20th century make it possible and necessary for managers at all levels to be productive, to grow effectively, and to realize great satisfaction and material reward from a career path that can also be strewn with pitfalls and danger.

Taoism is an ancient mystical teaching that can be traced back about 5,000 years. It emphasizes the harmonious development of physical, social, and spiritual elements of human life, and the self-realization of the whole being in ordinary life. Tao means "The Way," and I Ching or Te Ching means "The Book of Change." The I Ching has evolved from the contributions of philosophers through many centuries and the commentaries of scholars through the same period into a living work of great wisdom and real practical value to a student, or to you, a manager. By accepting and understanding the Way and achieving harmony with universal order, the manager exists in concert with his time and surroundings. A manager is better able to enlighten him or herself and others (associates, subordinates, superiors, government officials, customers, suppliers, to name a few) and to accomplish tasks. We might safely say that the teachings and the Way of the Tao speak directly to management through receptiveness to reality, unbiased understanding, timing of action and inaction, and avoidance of subjectivity and arbitrariness as a basis for action.

Management is task-oriented, whether commercial in nature or not. Today's manager is a "change manager" in a society that may be described as overly dependent on and fixated with technology and rapid rates of change. Therefore, the manager must develop his or her skills and insights to manage change while influencing its rate, direction, and extent. The path for developing these skills, awarenesses, and insights lies within oneself. For the important matters, a manager is on his or her own.

The career path of today's manager poses obstacles, dangers, and pitfalls along the way to success and self-realization. Burnout, family and marital problems, substance abuse, and the life-shortening results of stress are but a few of the "dangers to self" faced by a manager. Loss of job and diminished self-esteem through inadequate performance is ever present as a danger to one on the career path of management. The Tao enables a manager to tap his or her inner resources on the way to real success, human accomplishment, and satisfaction.

The Tao cautions against arrogance, materialism, insincerity, self-aggrandizement, and self-serving behavior. As managers, we have all seen these traits in people we consider "successful" and even "heroic," and wonder later why these self-serving behaviors are often so highly rewarded with material success and social acclaim.

The path of the Tao is deeply rooted in ethical behavior. A manager following this path will avoid the rapid rise and fall of the "flash-in-the-pan" hero. The path of the Tao in management is one of attainment, harmony, and of reaching one's potential. The ethical teachings of the Tao allow the manager to clearly establish a working value system in order to avoid the disasters faced by those who manage in a shallow, selfish, and overly forceful manner. Your greatest reward and satisfaction as a manager will be from a career that continues uninterruptedly to its highest potential. The resources you will call upon are those from within yourself, those which provide the skill and awareness to marshall your resources and those of your organization most productively. This is the path of the Tao.

The central feature of the I Ching is the hexagram, a pattern of six horizontal lines, to be read from the bottom upward. The hexagram is formed by the questioner in what, to western minds, seems a purely random manner, using yarrow stalks, coins, or wands. To the Chinese mind, though, there is nothing random about it: the pattern

3

formed is the unique and inevitable product of the moment, a finger-print of the questioner's predicament, bound up with and reflecting that person's past and future. The ancient users of the I Ching believed that spirits were communicating with them through the medium of chance, as expressed in the fall of the stalks, coins, or wands. Modern users may prefer C.G. Jung's explanation that it is the unconscious mind that is being consulted. Whichever view you prefer, the I Ching seems to have its own personality, one that accepts changing explanations with perfect equanimity, because the acceptance of change as the greatest natural law is the very basis of its philosophy. It is a guide to the world of flux in which we exist.

The History of the I Ching

Like many ancient books, the I Ching is the product of more than one hand. The I Ching has existed in some form for 4,000 years. It has meant many different things to different ages and cultures, which, in view of its name, ought not to surprise us. This book is more than a means of prediction; it is a book of wisdom that offers advice on how to cope with your present condition. It is the product of a culture different and more ancient than ours. The I Ching stress-es the fundamental Chinese approach to constant cyclical changes. It is a view of the universe as an entity in constant flux. In order to understand the I Ching, one needs to accept the ancient Chinese way of thinking about the world, especially on the subjects of change and chance. The two symbols used in the hexagram, the broken and unbroken lines, predate recorded history. They have thus long been ascribed to the mythical figure Fu Hsi, said to have been the first Emperor of China. The eight trigrams formed from them and found as the two halves of the hexagrams are said to have been discovered on the shell of a sacred tortoise. Two early books of change were used for divination under the Hsia Dynasty (2205-1766 B.C.) and the Shang Dynasty (1766-1150 B.C.), but the present set of 64 hexa-grams is said to have been compiled by King Wen (died c. 1150 BC). He also began the process of adding explanatory text, which was continued by his son, the Duke of Chou, to form an oracle that was used throughout the Chou Dynasty (1150-249 B.C.). This is thought to have been the form in which Confucius knew and studied it. Confucius is believed to have written one of the additional commentaries and, in time, the rest came to be attributed to him as well. In the next few centuries, there were many more textual accretions, only parts of which survive. Under the Ch'in (221-206 B.C.) and Han (206-220 A.D.) dynasties, the I Ching was practically submerged under a layer of magic and the Yin-Yang doctrine. A scholar called Wang Pi (226-249 A.D.) rescued it from these later interpretations and argued that it should be used as a fund of wisdom, not merely a means of divining the future. It then developed into a guide to statecraft. Present texts are based on the early 18th century A.D. edition called Chou I Che Chung. In the west, the most widely used translations have been those of James Legge (into English, 1899) and Richard Wilhelm (into German, 1924, and then into English).

Lao Tsu and Taoism

Lao Tsu was an older contemporary of Confucius. He was keeper of the imperial archives at Loyang in the province of Honan in the sixth century B.C. All his life, he taught that "the Tao that can be told is not the eternal Tao." The essence of Taoism is contained in the 81 chapters of the Tao Teh Ching, which is a major influence in Chinese thought and culture. Where Confucius was concerned with daily rules for living in a civilized way, Taoism is concerned more with spiritual aspects of being.

Lao Tzu's Tao Teh Ching is one of the most translated works in the world. Its pages contain simple, yet profound, truths. Taoists consider Lao Tzu to be the greatest teacher of all time. He is regarded as a sage, and legend states that he spent 81 years in his mother's womb. As the emperor's librarian and keeper of the Royal Archives, Lao Tzu came into contact with the works of China's greatest sages writing before 2700 B.C. He became aware that a time of great confusion and spiritual disintegration was to befall the empire. He decided to leave society and live a life of seclusion in harmony with nature. Thus he rode westward on the back of a water buffalo. When he came to the Han Gu Pass at the border of China, he was requested by the pass official to write down the essence of his wisdom. This classic has since been called the Tao Teh Ching.

Lao Tzu traveled on and continued to share his teachings with those who sought to live according to the Tao. Only one known compilation of those later teachings, known as the Hua Hu Ching, has survived. During the Yuan Dynasty, the emperor Shuen Ti (1333 A.D.-1367 A.D.) was persuaded by religious leaders of that time to ban the Hua Hu Ching and order all copies of the book to be burned. Buddhists felt that their spiritual leader, Sakyamuni, was degraded by the Hua Hu Ching, because many associated him with the Prince who appears as Lao Tzu's student in the book. The influence of the book can be seen in the later teachings of the Buddha. The Ch'an school of Chinese Buddhism and Zen Buddhism in Japan are derived from ancient Taoist teachings. The Hua Hu Ching is a very rare manuscript, even in China. The teachings contained in the Hua Hu Ching survived only through generation after generation of Taoist masters.

The teachings of Lao Tzu are both rational and spiritual. Like water, they are fluid, yet their power is immeasurable. They are the expression of utmost simplicity and purest wisdom. Truth itself is power. Many recorded anecdotes reveal another realm of life that is pointed to in the teachings of Lao Tzu. A book can be burned by those who fear spiritual development, but none can destroy its truths.

Confucius

Confucius lived from 552 to 479 B.C. His name was more properly K'ung-fu-tzu, and he came from the state of Lu in the south of what is now the Shantung province of China. Although he is commonly thought of as a scholar and writer, he in fact devoted more time to formulating and teaching an ethical theory of statecraft. His aim was to see his humane reforms applied in his lifetime, but he was denied any influential post and had to transfer his hopes to the careers of his pupils. Yet his teachings, although encrusted with wrongly attributed texts and dubious reinterpretations, eventually came to dominate the thought of China for 2,000 years. He undoubtedly studied the I Ching and is said to have remarked that if he could have his life extended he would devote 50 years to it and thereby avoid many errors. It came to be regarded as one of the classics of Confucianism, but his authorship of most of the commentaries is now disputed.

Yin and Yang

The circular symbol design is common in Chinese art as a symbol of the trigrams in never-ending interaction about the emblem of Yang and Yin. The unbroken line began as a simple sign for "yes" in divination. It is now called Yang, heaven, or "the firm," and is associated with the positive, active, and masculine side of nature. The broken line stood at first for "no," and is now called Yin, earth, "the yielding," and is linked with the negative, feminine, passive side of nature.

Yin and Yang, the two primordial forces that govern the universe, symbolize harmony. They are opposites: Yin is dark, Yang is light; Yin is passive, Yang is active; Yin is female, Yang is male. All things contain varying degrees of Yin and Yang. Yin and Yang continually interact, creating cyclical change. Yin and Yang merge together into one, naturally and constantly creating Tao, the universal situation.

Ch'i, the breath of life, is man's aura, man's real self, his energy and soul. It propels us through life and affects our interactions with others. Every human movement influences both the self and other people. We are drawn together and repelled as magnets attract and repel. People are also sensitive to the ch'i of the environment. Environmental ch'i shapes human ch'i, casting man's destiny.

The Trigrams

Trigrams are formed from three broken or unbroken lines, and each
sort of line has significance at various levels. The lines are grouped
in threes in every possible permutation, making eight Trigrams in all.

Each Trigram has a name and is further elucidated by an attribute, an
image, and a family relationship. Remember that the Trigrams are
regarded as symbols of change, not as a set of static conditions and
that one Trigram is constantly changing into another.

Each of the eight Trigrams combines the two types of
line in a different way, ranging from the complete dom-
inance of Yang to the supremacy of Yin. The Trigram
is read from the bottom up.

Each Trigram is named with a Chinese character. Each
Trigram also has an attribute revealing the kind of
action that is indicated by the particular combination of
lines.

Images are also associated with the eight Trigrams.
They include heaven and earth and all the major fea-
tures and phenomena that occur between the two.

Certain relationships from within the family are linked
with the Trigrams. The masculine usually is associated
with movement, the feminine with devotion.

The eight Trigrams can be combined into 64
Hexagrams, each of which are constructed from two
Trigrams. The primary goal of this book is the interpretation of these Hexagrams in the context of management concerns and decisions.

The Hexagrams are shown below, arranged in order
from Yang on the lower right to Yin on the upper left.

8

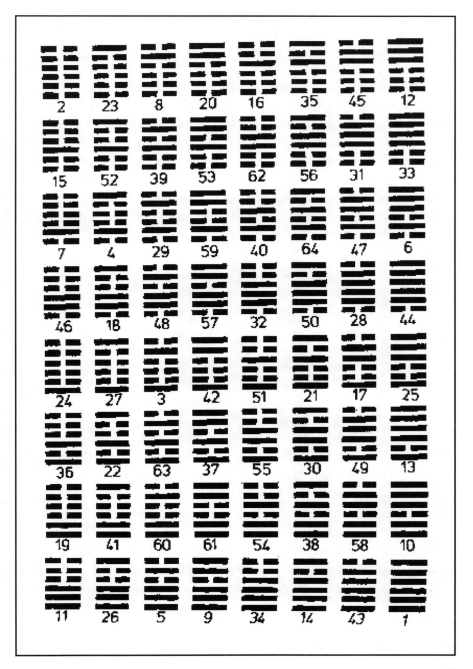

Generating the Hexagrams

1. Select three farite coins for exclusive use when making your enquiry. Avoid letting others handle your coins and always put them away safely.

2. Clear your mind of distractions, preferably in a quiet, private place. While manipulating the coins, formulate a question that will force you to explore and examine the conditions surrounding the situation of interest, and designate in your own mind whether you are the active or passive party.

3. Write down the exact time and date and your specific question. If you wish, you can designate specific lines for particular types of information you seek.

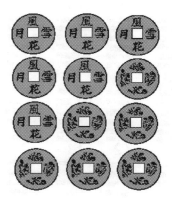

4. When you are ready, toss all three coins at once. The first toss determines the bottom line of the Hexagram. There are four types of lines.

5. Toss the coins a total of six times. Draw each line above the preceeding one until you have drawn a Hexagram consisting of six lines. This Hexagram represents the present situation.

As you toss the coins, put a small mark beside any line that comes up three of a kind. These are known as the moving lines. If none of the lines is a moving line, it indicates that the present situation is static, at least for now.

6. If you received any moving lines, draw a second future Hexagram next to the first one, directly transferring the static lines, but converting the moving lines to their opposites. This second Hexagram represents the future situation.

7. There is also a hidden, inner Hexagram which indicates the underlying influences or root cause of the present situation. It often sets the mood for the present Hexagram. Many of the cryptic references in the text are derived from the symbols found in the inner Hexagram. This third Hexagram is derived by removing the top and bottom lines and stretching out the remaining superimposed lines.

II
Interpretation of The Hexagrams

1. Ch'ien

Creative action is favored. There is an emphasis on origins and development. Be watchful for an opportunity to move forward in positive, firm action. This is an extremely advantageous time to begin or persevere on a creative course.

Ch'ien: Heaven over Heaven

Creative

The creative represents the strength of the Tao, you, and your organization.

Strength is born, expanded, fulfilled, and consolidated. If any of these aspects of strength are lacking, the creative quality of strength is not complete.

The manager must never confuse strength with force. They are not the same.

The manager concentrates on the accomplishment of his or her tasks and is minimally visible.

Arrogance is the extreme of knowing something about winning but nothing about losing. Arrogance blocks a manager by diminishing creative strength.

2. K'un

By remaining correct and steadfast, advantage will arise. Stay receptive and flexible while keeping firm to a goal. Seeking guidance, listening, and waiting are favored. The symbol of the mare is associated with this hexagram, as the mare is gentle and docile, yet strong. Creation and development will come through being receptive and patient.

K'un: Earth over Earth

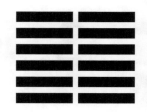

Receptive

Receptive is the nature of one who serves. It is the station of second place.

Management is a service to the organization. The manager becomes receptive, yielding, devoted, moderate, and correct.

The receptive mind is obedient to natural principles and is able to develop understanding from confusion.

The manager makes things right, strives for fulfillment of his or her duty, and completes tasks without fabrication.

3. Chun

*Staying true to one course through difficulty
will lead to success. It is not necessary to take
immediate action; progress comes from staying
firm, correct, and faithful. Great development
comes from perseverance and asking for assistance. In the beginning stages of any action,
there is bound to be difficulty. Progress does
not come to those who turn away, avoid, or
ignore the obstacles all around.*

Chun: Water over Thunder

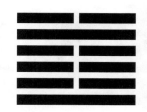

Difficulty at the Beginning

All beginnings are complicated and difficult.
Difficulty naturally arises when the creative and receptive unite to create.

A manager's success in dealing with difficulty at the beginning is achieved through perseverance, delaying decisions, and asking for assistance.

The confusion of difficulty will result in order.

The manager pursues goals within a prevailing mood of hesitation and hindrance. He or she becomes subordinate to inferiors so that the hearts of all can be won. In this case, correctness of management style in dealing with difficulty allows for creativity and results in success.

4. Meng

The warm and nurturing force of earth is doubled and intensified. The receptive nature of earth provides growth.

Meng: Mountain over Wind

Darkness

Darkness comes from using intellect mistakenly, thereby reducing cleverness.

This artificial cleverness results in the seeking of a reality which is already there.

A manager must be open, calm, sincere, and serious. He or she proceeds along the path of noncontrivance.

The innocence of action needed in the midst of darkness is the innocence which is cognizant of darkness.

Darkness is a confusion which moves the manager on to subsequent enlightenment.

5. Hsu

The tranquil water is disturbed by turbulence below, creating storms, obstacles, and adverse conditions. Only a steady course will lead out of dangerous waters.

Hsu: Water over Heaven

Waiting

A manager who is sound and strong and able to manage in the midst of danger is "waiting." Waiting is nurturing.

Do not presume upon your supposed strength. Do not hope on the remote chance of luck.

Awareness of danger requires care, caution, the refining of one's self, and the awaiting of the proper time.

When the proper time arrives, after waiting, a manager acts in an appropriate way.

A manager is strong and cognizant of danger.

6. Sung

In contention there is sincerity; obstructed, be careful to be balanced, for that will lead to good results. Finality leads to bad results. It is beneficial to see a great person, not beneficial to cross great rivers. Contention arises because of need. Combine desire and strength. It is imperative to be fully sincere and truthful, or contention leads to mere intrigue and misfortune. Choose a secure place and stay there.

Sung: Heaven over Water

Contention

Arguments, battles of wit, and issues of right and wrong are behaviors that deviate from harmony.

They result in a loss of balance for the manager, the team, and the entire organization.

In following the path of the Tao, a manager becomes acutely aware of his or her temperament and the nature of that temperament which is most harmful.

Caution and moderation are tempered by inner strength and the holding back of outward aggressiveness. A manager does not seek outside justice.

Winning an argument is not the same thing as getting the job done.

7. Shih

For the firm to be right, mature people are good; then there is no fault. Go along obediently with the firm. The cause must be right. Even if the firm acts correctly, the leaders must be mature to obtain good results. Be lucky and faultless-mature, stern, and worthy of respect.

Shih: Earth over Water

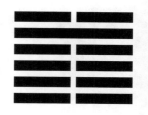

Militancy

In militancy, the manager chooses the way to punishment and execution, command, and authority... and
needs the ability to change in order to be effective.

When there is peace, the military manager, even the
great military leader, is not needed.

It is not always possible to restore peace in perilous
times.Those who disturb are often brought forth by
forceful management.

A manager in times of militancy proceeds in an
orderly manner. Ignorant actions result in casualties
and loss of valuable associates and outside allies.

Sometimes, a judicious retreat can avoid mistakes.

When order is restored, there is no longer need for
punishment and execution. The manager then rewards
meritorious achievement and chastises those of little or
no merit.

8. Pi

Whenever there is a group, there is closeness, which means friendly assistance. People should be friendly and assist each other; only then can there be peace and security. When people are friendly and based in truth, closeness naturally becomes a way to good fortune. Figure out with whom to associate closely. Persevere, be steadfast. No one can survive alone, not even the strong. Do not cling out of weakness; this brings misfortune.

Pi: Water over Earth

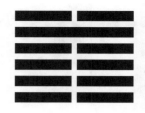

Accord

A manager must achieve union and accord with what is right and real and must be assured inwardly that this accord is based in true reality.

A manager must have an open mind and be willing to give in order to receive. True accord and union with those around you can only come from within.

Further, the manager is known by his or her associates. Union with ignorant and foolish people will reflect poorly.

True accord calls for leadership. A manager should indeed approach a true leader or teacher. There is nothing wrong with asking for help and/or guidance.

9. Hsiao Ch'u

In closeness, nurturance must develop. Gather into a group. When close, peoples' aims build from each other. Stabilize, assemble. Nothing is better than to develop and stabilize firm strength with flexibility. Heaven below, wind above. Small development is successful. Opposites come together and form one group.

Hsiao Ch'u: Wind over Heaven

Nurturance by the Small

Management from the lower levels is developmental, but can mean small development for the organization and the people in it.

However, a manager who walks with and among his or her people knows greatness and is humble. A manager grows through humility.

This should represent valuable insight and should be thought over in the spirit of honest self-evaluation.

10. Lu

After people live together and develop, there are manners, conduct. Act on and be acted upon. Firmness acts upon flexibility. Live a life worthy of humanity. One uses flexibility to bear firmness. Living naturally, avoid injury.

Lu: Heaven over Lake

Treading

Treading means forward progress.

A manager needs firmness of purpose here and must operate with strength of mind, robust energy, and sincerity.

In treading, avoid impetuous action because ignorance and incompetence can only bring misfortune.

A manager practices self-mastery in times of peril.

11. T'ai

When conduct is serene, one is at peace. Acts are in their places. Get through and be secure. The small goes, the great comes; auspicious success. Harmony. When the leadership delegates tasks and the workers do their tasks as best they can and the wills of those above and those below communicate, the result is tranquility for the central hub of an organization. Ups and downs come in cycles with time.

T'ai: Earth over Heaven

Tranquility

This is developmental in that the small goes and the great comes and the organization goes through in harmony.

There is proper timing in the course of work.

Proper timing in taking advantage of opportunity can bring about tranquility.

Tranquility can be lost by softness. The balanced and flexible manager can bring opposition into submission.

Manage strongly while acting in a docile manner so as to nurture your strength wisely.

A primary goal for managers is to bring about and preserve harmony.

12. P'i

Tranquility cannot last forever; obstruction follows. Things come and go. Heaven and earth are separated and do not communicate. Obstruction negates humanity.

P'i: Heaven over Earth

Obstruction

Obstruction always exists in opposition to harmony. Through obstruction, the great goes and the small comes.

The manager's goal is to effect balance immediately. Hiding embarrassment or just being unaware means that the manager does not know that there is obstruction or blockage in the organization.

In times of organizational or individual blockage, it is helpful and even necessary to go back and start over. The manager reverses the flow of events and restores tranquility.

The manager must be aware of the path of events which surround him or her.

13. T'ung Jen

Association with others is successful. The correctness of developed people is beneficial. Association with others in the countryside is free from regret.

T'ung Jen: Heaven over Fire

Fellowship and Assimilation

Fellowship and assimilation are brought out by the character of the manager, not by his or her position.

A manager must skillfully and sincerely mix and assimilate with others. This true sameness with others is developmental.

Do not be a fair-weather manager. Be true in good times and in bad.

The manager must always recognize that there are people with whom he or she should not assimilate. Assimilation as a management technique is based upon correctness and other rational factors, never on emotion.

True mutuality exists as a result of truly natural and productive activity. The manager develops his or her self inwardly while at the same time developing others outwardly.

This is the condition within which the manager is able to adapt to change and set truly significant goals.

14. Ta Yu

Things come to those who associate with others. Honor, flexibility, everyone trusts.

Ta Yu: Fire over Heaven

Great Possessions

Great possessions represent the success and reward brought about through management efforts and effective work.

The manager must be firm and flexible, so that which is great now will grow greater. The manager always builds on strength.

This individual and organizational condition requires nurturing within and the repudiation of adornments.

Daily rewards call for daily renewal by the manager.

15. Ch'ien

Remain lowly even when great, having great possessions. Have virtue without dwelling upon it. Do not compete. Inwardly fulfilled, defer to others and be not proud. This leads to more respect from others. Petty people compete and are proud. Leaders are hardworking, yet humble. Command respect.

Ch'ien: Earth over Mountain

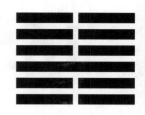

Humility

Humility is having great possessions and not dwelling upon them.

Lacking humility, a manager and his or her organization become empty, disrespectful, and lazy.

Humility is recognized by its quality and endurance. It should be practiced in both favorable and unfavorable situations.

True humility enriches all. Satiety brings on resentment.

The manager humbly follows the strong, is hard-working, and extends his humility to the high and to the low.

Do not underrate the positive effect of true humility.

16. Yu

Even if possessions are great, one can be humble. Harmonious enjoyment, docile activity. Delight makes it advantageous to set up overseers and mobilize the army. Obedient action, receptivity. Follow who or what delights you. Overseers set up stability, are harmonious and accommodating. Accomplishment follows. Act compliantly.

Yu: Thunder over Earth

Joy and Enthusiasm

Joy results from the possession of something great when there is humility.

No manager should be foolish enough in this rejoicing to associate with petty people.

Joy in the organization can lead to inertia.

A manager pursues his or her own true path and not merely personal desires.

The manager is in accord with the Tao lest joy be lost.

This joy of gain is achieved through the manager's use of firm strength.

17. Sui

Following is very successful, beneficial if correct, then blameless. Communications outside have great merit. Have sincerity; use understanding on the path and there is no fault.

Sui: Lake over Thunder

Following

Following is developmental. Others rejoice when one acts. The manager is fulfilling the expectations of others.

By following along the path of what is desired, the manager has the opportunity of gradually introducing guidance. He or she identifies times for action and stillness and other times for advance and withdrawal.

It should not be necessary to remind one that following requires great care in the beginning.

Weak following results in a loss of reality and then a loss in everything else.

Following can result in strength only by abiding in right and not moving-and by following while trusting in goodness.

As a manager, it is unreasonable to expect others to follow you before you have followed them.

The Tao cautions against ignorance and excess.

18. Ku

There is a mishap. Disorder and decay follow. When there is degeneration, there is great success. Restoration may follow. Government exists because of disorder. When degeneration is great, the difficulty of finding a remedy presents dangerous obstacles. Figuring out the context of the origin is the way to remedy decadence and to endure. To achieve long-term results, reflect upon what course of action to take.

Ku: Mountain over Wind

Degeneration

The manager encounters degeneration following joy and enthusiasm and knows that human and organizational degeneration are preconditions for repair.

The manager returns to fundamentals from which the path of repair will follow. He or she knows that action will be called for, since degeneration cannot be corrected in a setting of empty tranquility.

This action places the manager in a setting of danger and difficulty.

One must not be excessively adamant or weak in correction-and had better know whether things are degenerating or not.

Often, this is the time to utilize the strength and clarity of others to break down one's own ignorance and restore things to a state of nondegeneration.

Fame and profit are not your targets here. Spiritual values and virtues allow for nondegeneration.

Great progress for the manager and his or her organization results from dealing effectively with degeneration.

19. Lin

With people and affairs, take the sense of those above, oversee. Benefit from correctness. Confusion is coming. Be careful and prevent fullness to make it endure. Do not relax and indulge.

Lin: Earth over Lake

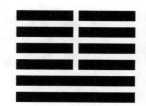

Supervising

Supervising is the heart and the core of managing.

Supervising is both creative and developmental wherein the process becomes increasingly manifest and expands.

All systems are "go", and negative factors are repressed.

The manager avoids negligence and eagerness. He or she identifies appropriate opportunities and takes advantage of them in a correct manner.

When supervision is creative and developmental, there is no obstruction.

Do not look for "quick fixes." Moving ahead too quickly results in sudden regression.

A manager always seeks guidance and help.

Supervision is an ultimate expression of management, and the result is completion of both the beginning and the end.

20. Kuan

Watch. Human leaders observe the courses of above and below. Cultivate virtues to carry out government, be admired by the people. The washing of the hands without presentation of the offering holds sincere reverence. Dignity before action.

Kuan: Wind over Earth

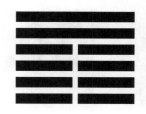

Observing

The manager is always an alert and careful observer.

Observation requires clarity of mind and is closely tied to degeneration.

Alert observation is the path for correcting degeneration.

Sincerity will gain the manager acceptance and success. Inward truthfulness dissipates acquired influences.

Receptiveness and quick action rely on management's skills and observation. Do not accept the false and reject the real.

This is a time for the manager to examine his or her own growth and the growth of others.

Build upon strength.

21. Shih Ho

Joining in action becomes necessary when there are people or things standing in the way; worldly affairs do not come together harmoniously. Cut through to peace and order. Treachery causes a rift; eliminate it to achieve cooperation and order. Supervisory custody, not punishment, is a means of thorough observation to see what is true and what is false. Preventative measures can then be used in the future.

Shih Ho: Fire over Thunder

Decisiveness

Decisiveness is acting with unfailing clarity and clear understanding. It is good managing.

A manager can only practice what he or she clearly and thoroughly understands. The quality of action is based on understanding.

Decisiveness is "biting through" the entirety of a situation and not "nibbling" around the edges or just "pulling off" what is loose around the bone.

Decisiveness requires and demands true understanding.

The manager disregards falsehood and keeps truth.

22. Pi

When people associate with each other, there is culture; culture is adornment. Standards of conduct and ranks of status exist within a group. Order and organization illuminate the patterns above. Contribute to getting somewhere. One cannot take a stand without a basis, one cannot act without culture. Adorn substance to get success. Add luster, color and refinement. Make prosperity evident.

Pi: Mountain over Fire

Adornment

Adornment represents beautification.

In managing through observing, we arrive at a condition wherein clarity becomes stabilized.

Clarity and stillness adorn each other. A manager does not let stillness degenerate into quietness.

The manager values clarity as a place of rest and stillness. One should not use it lightly as the clarity of illumination.

Adornment itself is developmental but results in progress when not overdone.

The manager expands knowledge and wisdom at this time. Shutting out external artifice, he or she does not allow adornment and luxuriance to hinder clarity of understanding.

Real adornment is the mutuality of clarity and stillness and is a means by which the work of hidden cultivation and quiet practice is not clouded.

23. Po

Climax is adornment followed by reversion. Stripping away does not make it beneficial to go anywhere. Petty people tear down enlightened people. Speak in an agreeable manner, conceal your doings, and act according to the time so as to escape being harmed by petty people.

Po: Mountain over Earth

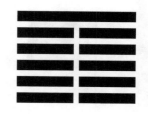

Stripping Away

Stripping away is disposing of everything and thereby having nothing left.

The manager who follows his or her desires and can only press forward and cannot step back winds up losing basic essence. Eating the fruit and throwing away the pit causes disaster.

While stripping away is most easily described in material and financial terms, its greatest impact to the manager is in the human and spiritual areas.

24. Fu

When stripping away concludes, there is rebirth. The path of enlightened leadership fades away and returns to what is good. When companions come, there is no fault. Arrive at full growth, end the suppression of action. Leaders can lead again, followers can follow. A reasonable course of action can be found. Energy becomes available to start on the path of good starts.

Fu: Earth over Thunder

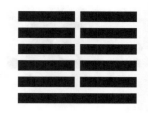

Return

Return means coming back and is developmental.

It is necessary to know the timing of the return, not to seek return forcibly at the wrong time and definitely not to miss a timely opportunity.

The manager must pay close attention to return since it necessitates pursuing work in an orderly fashion.

Good must be restored gradually since immediate restoration is inherently unstable.

While return is always possible for the manager and the organization, it is hindered when one is deceived by personal desires and confused by outside influences.

There is great growth for the manager in return, but one must be careful in the beginning.

Unstable return requires repetition. The single-minded manager moves through perilous times and returns many times.

This last has to do with the manager's learning, losing, and striving diligently.

25. Wu Wang

Returning to the Way, you have no error. Keep in accordance with true reason. Heaven above, movement below, acting through the celestial. Great success. Be correct. It is not beneficial to go anywhere. Perfect truthfulness. If one does not accord with true reason, then one errs. Work from the "center."

Wu Wang: Heaven over Thunder

Fidelity

A manager conducts him or herself with whole-hearted sincerity and is creative and developmental without duplicity.

Fidelity is genuine.

The manager puts aside external influences while acting in a timely manner, utilizing the appropriate strength.

Do not follow the contrivances of your mind and wrongfully seek treasure.

You must give before you can receive.

The benefits of true fidelity can be great-and so also can be the misfortunes.

26. Ta Ch'u

Buildup and stopping. Learning and virtue build up to fullness within. Once this happens, it is appropriate to be in a high position. Receive sustenance from heaven and distribute it to the world to help others out of difficulty.

Ta Ch'u: Mountain over Heaven

Nurturance of the Great

The manager nurtures and develops restored energy to make it greater, more indestructible and incorruptible.

One's strength is stilled while on this path so that it can be nurtured and grow.

This is a path without force.

Greatness of nurturance results in great development.

Strength is balanced, stabilized, and developed to its highest level, a level of consummation. Improperly promoted strength brings misfortune here.

Strength is to be nurtured at the beginning.

A manager treads this path with single-mindedness and a full, complete spirit.

27. I

People nourish life, the body, and virtue. Appropriate regulation of activity and rest is necessary. Quality of behavior and performance of duty increase. Extend your concern for self to others; nourish people.

I: Mountain over Thunder

Nourishment

In nourishment, action and stillness become unified.

The manager chooses and holds fast to the good and seeks fulfillment through emptiness.

Inwardly observing truth and falseness, the manager nourishes the right and is rid of the wrong.

Nourishment, like fulfillment, must be sought by a manager looking inward, emptying the mind of irrelevant things.

Be careful in the beginning. Do not act in ignorance or be distracted by human desire and folly.

28. Ta Kuo

The virtues and accomplishments of the wise greatly surpass those of others. The Way, always constant and centered, is not commonly seen by others and greatly surpasses the ordinary. It is beneficial to go; you will get somewhere.

Ta Kuo: Lake over Thunder

Excess

The manager must be careful in dealing with excess and not indulge in it.

For instance, great strength can do great damage when used to excess. The damage will accrue to the practitioner.

Avoid the excessive use of strength by knowing how and when to withdraw.

Excessive weakness is as negative as excessive strength.

Harmony, adaptability, avoiding danger, and being aware of perils imbue the manager with the firmness and flexibility to avoid excess.

Excess of the great can never be one-sided or partial. The manager will do well to recognize this so as not to directly or indirectly bring about great misfortune.

29. K'an

Redoubled danger; danger within danger. If there is sincerity, this mind will get through with worthy action. Have sincerity and truthfulness within; wholeheartedness. If one does not act, one will always remain in danger.

K'an: Water over Water

Pitfalls

Pitfalls are danger.

A manager must know how to get through danger. The path of practice is followed-it is the practice of good, the way out of danger.

In order to remove oneself from danger, one must believe in the danger.

Belief rules the mind of the manager. This belief avoids distraction and allows the practice of good.

There is great simplicity in the belief in danger and the need for practice to get out of danger. This is developmental and of great benefit to the manager and the organization.

A manager who repeats pitfalls and continually lives in peril is self-destructive.

30. Li

One has fallen into danger and difficulty and must cling to something. Fire means clinging, but it also means light. The center is open. Clinging is beneficial if correct. Cling to people, way of life, work. Cling to something correct. Follow the right Way in a docile manner.

Li: Fire over Fire

Fire

Fire is cleansing, illuminating, and beneficial for correctness and development.

A manager's development is assisted by fire only if the use and nurturing of its illumination is known. It is the inner illumination referred to here, which is the basis for other illumination.

Illumination (inner and outer) results in open awareness, clarity, and action in the path of good. Illuminated work is correct and results in good fortune. The manager must seek illumination constantly in order to use it.

When not illuminated, the manager is aware and seeks illumination from others. This opens the mind, produces understanding, and turns weakness into strength. Nurture illumination to avoid trouble arising from excess. The manager who only deals with outer illumination becomes weak, incapable, and impotent in action.

From a management point of view, knowing one is not illuminated is reparable.

31. Hsien

Feelings based on joy arise. Constancy is consistency and is based on correctness. Harmony in action, firmness, and flexibility-this is joy. Youth, earnest communication, sincerity; joy responds.

Hsien: Lake over Mountain

74

Sensitivity

Sensitivity means feeling and influence. It represents harmony.

The path of sensitivity has the potential for being equally developmental or perilous.

The manager must move with true spontaneity and ignore outside influences and human desires. Failure to achieve a genuine condition of sensitivity results in humiliation.

Clever words and external artificialities do not represent true sensitivity.

32. Heng

Marriage is the path of sensing and is constant. Hardness is above and softness below. Be active and gentle. Respond to one another. Constancy gets through without blame, is beneficial when correct. It is beneficial to go somewhere. Persevere continually to reach a goal. Go towards something constantly. Fixed things must change. Blamelessness, movement, forward action.

Heng: Thunder over Wind

Constancy

Constancy has to do with long persistence and genuine application. It is sound management practice.

While fire involves inward and outward illumination aimed at profound attainment of personal realization, constancy orients the manager toward the single-minded application of the will. The manager is not lazy and does not slack off. This can be a strong and positive path of development.

We all see managers and associates who are capable of constancy but are constant along deviant paths. They seek success in this manner, but rather hasten their personal and professional demise. Correct constancy moves the manager to thoroughly penetrate different kinds of truths.This is a path of action for the manager, for without action there is no constancy.

Empty evaluation and self-aggrandizement are inevitably followed by ruin, as the culmination of elevation is inevitably followed by a fall.

Fooling oneself is poor management practice and is not the path of the Tao.

33. Tun

Retreat. Escape, departure, leaving. Withdrawal gets you through. It is beneficial to be correct in small things. Enlightened people withdraw into hiding. Negative weakness is growing, but not yet widespread. Enlightened people still have a way to make efforts slowly. The enlightened way is obscured; use caution and withdraw. Do not be righteous over great matters, be correct in small things.

Tun: Heaven over Mountain

Withdrawal

The manager withdraws when he retracts, using strength with restraint.

This is developmental for the manager and keeps external influences from wasting energy.

Care in the beginning is yet again cautioned by the Tao.

Avoid personal entanglements by not acting arbitrarily.

The manager subdues energy and accepts the truth.

This is a path where strength and flexibility act equally, allowing the manager freedom and independence.

This is an individual management choice.

34. Ta Chuang

Progress, growth. Flourishing follows the decline. Phases of cyclical processes are interdependent. Strength and movement. Act with strength. Caution: use in the right; otherwise, it is just mere force.

Ta Chuang: Thunder over Heaven

Great Power

Great power is ceaseless internal strength and efficacy in action. This is why it is called great power. The manager with great power experiences extraordinary direction in life and does what others cannot do. He or she transcends the ordinary and accomplishes the rare.

Deviation from the path of theTao, ignorance of danger, ignorance of reality, and avoidance of change can result in the harming of life by power. There is then no value in power. The manager who follows this path without care and prudence at the beginning risks the consequences of failure, danger, and peril. Great power must be kept in balance by the fortunate manager who possesses it. Self-mastery allows this manager to have inwardly more than enough strength and to be powerful without being excessively so.

Weakness without firm strength makes it impossible for the manager (or the organization) to be vigorous even though the time and situation call for vigor. The weak and incapable seek a teacher.

Studying, practicing, and working intensely while struggling intensely is becoming powerful by resorting to what is right.

35. Chin

Once one has power, advancement follows. Light emerges from the earth. Progress and great illumination abound. A time of progress toward fulfillment is coming. Rulership is enlightened. The leadership is illuminated and the subordinates are obedient, so the directorate and the administration suit each other. Fullness of illumination brings high distinction and glory to the administration.

Chin: Fire over Earth

Advance

Advancing is management progress which is based on understanding and growing illumination.

The manager restores illumination to the darkness of the closed mind through obedience, timing, and truth.

Seek illumination when it is not advanced, and do not rush to promote it in the midst of darkness. Seek the illumination of others when necessary.

The manager is secure while in a state of tranquility and peace.

There is no management situation in which one cannot use illumination and there is no place that can damage true illumination.

36. Ming I

Darkness. Ignorant leadership is in power and illuminatees get injured. Light is destroyed. It is beneficial to be upright in difficulty. Know the difficulties and remain true. Remember the path through the darkness.

Ming I: Earth over Fire

Concealment of Illumination

Where being strong in action results in advance without withdrawal, power is excessive and injures the manager's illumination.

The manager does not conceal his or her illumination in a most secret place and does not use it lightly.

The nurturing of inward and outward illumination allows it to be free of defect.

When illumination does not penetrate reality, injury is caused. This injury causes the manager to withdraw and conceal the illumination.

Outward hurt does not mean inward hurt. Withdraw and conceal illumination when damage is suffered.

This is the "damage control" of the Tao and is good management practice.

Illumination is to be nurtured, stored, and available

37. Chia Jen

Hurt on the outside, go home to the way of family life, affection among family members. Duty and order live there. Be ethically correct and earnest in social obligations. One's own fire comes from within. Inwardly understanding while outwardly conforming is the way to manage the home. Managing a home or organization, extend the former to the latter.

Chia Jen: Wind over Fire

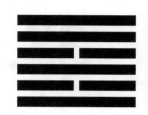

Inner Governance

The manager refines his or her self, masters the mind, and turns attention around to gaze inward.

By not being firm in refinement, the manager allows laziness, trickiness, and self-indulgence to destroy order. He or she is humiliated.

Balance here unifies firmness and flexibility and allows one to seek out and pursue the path of gentility toward a purpose of selflessness.

Self-governance, selflessness, and the refinement of the inner self is a serious matter.

38. K'uei

When the Way of the family ends, there is alienation. Going different ways, different aims and goals. Small matters turn out well. Opposition and backing up are not on a fortunate path. But potential is good; even in time of disharmony, small matters turn out well.

K'uei: Fire over Lake

Disharmony

All managers face mutual opposition and know that it is best settled when it first arises.

It also can be settled correctly when it is in full force. The manager must bring union from disharmony. The mind must restore the light from within.

When this is done and desires are swept away and feelings are forgotten, it is possible to reconcile disharmony.

Disharmony can be caused by oneself where no disharmony has existed. The manager damages the inward by striving for the outward, by accepting the false. There is an end but no beginning.

Regret is useful in settling disharmony only if you regret in the beginning and at the end.

Take care with whom you associate. Associate with the right people because there is disharmony in solitude. Do not manage in a vacuum.

Most importantly, settle disharmony in the open, take advantage of timing, and use the settlement of small matters to correct disharmony in large ones.

39. Chien

Obstruction by danger. Pitfall and impasse. It is beneficial to see great people. It bodes well to be steadfast. Follow along easily; it is not advantageous to stop in danger. Difficulty can be resolved. Have wise people present to save the world from trouble, those with complete correctness who are steadfast in the true. Maintain upright behavior.

Chien: Water over Mountain

Halting

A manager halts, stopping in the midst of danger.

Forward progress is difficult here because the extreme of danger has burdened the inner mind with external influence.

Halting allows the manager to deal with and leave danger.

The manager controls danger by stillness and solves danger by action.

Stillness and action are both functions of the mind of Tao.

The manager is careful in halting when weakness is present.

Seeking guidance from others and forming associations with correct people broaden the manager's knowledge and wisdom.

The manager is best counseled to follow the Tao by being firm and not getting into trouble in the first place.

40. Hsieh

Movement over danger, thunder over water. Clouds clear. When there is nowhere to go, come back. When there is somewhere to go, be early. Refine governing, restoration comes after solution. Preventative measures. Return to right reason. If it is not eliminated early on, then a difficulty will grow again.

Hsieh: Thunder over Water

Liberation and Freedom

Sound management practice calls for taking advantage of the right time.

Returning without going anywhere does not come about through human effort. It appears spontaneously at a given time and comes from nature.When nature's time arrives, however, human exertion is necessary.

The manager must use inner resources to be liberated from danger and difficulty-and to be able to act freely as he or she wants. While promptness brings good fortune, tardiness here will result in failure. Liberation can be achieved regardless of one's condition.

When weak and helpless, and while danger is extreme, associate with the right people and borrow their strength. Adamance alone does not create sufficient force to liberate. Being strong will not do the job where weakness is present.

The balance between looseness and tightness is the liberation of Tao which sublimates all difficulty.

Timing, knowledge, illumination, and true recognition make the difference between management success and failure.

41. Sun

Solution...relaxation...something is lost. Work gladly for superiors. Reduction or loss, profit from those below. Reduction with sincerity is very auspicious. It is beneficial to go somewhere. Balance, not too much or too little. Get rid of errors to get into balance, back to basics. Truthful seriousness is at the base. Excess desires are rooted in developing implications too far. Reduce desire to return to the origins and basics.

Sun: Mountain over Lake

Reduction

A manager diminishes that which is excessive, thereby increasing accomplishment.

Practically speaking, there are few more important things to a manager than finishing those tasks which have been started.

This is a very positive and subtle practice in management.

Wrath, cupidity, and other disruptive conditions eat away at the natural reality of task and goals.

To practice reduction on a daily basis is to increase daily accomplishment.

Care at the beginning, conscientious reduction, and sincerity result in spontaneous increase in strength and perfection of beginning and end.

42. I

Growth follows decline. Decrease follows increase, like a circle. When those below are rich, those above are secure. Increase is beneficial with somewhere to go. Increase means the way to profit everyone. Resolve danger.

I: Wind over Thunder

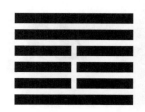

Increase

Effective management adds to and augments what is lacking on both individual and organizational levels.

The goal here is to eliminate compulsive habits.

This constitutes management of self; increasing through reducing the fundamental management process of constant beginnings and conclusions.

There is no need here to elaborate on the effect of beginnings without endings, or of the risk and peril of assisting others before developing oneself.

Management is always "self-management" first.

"Do as I say, not as I do" is not the path of the Tao.

43. Kuai

Continual increase follows. Use firm decisiveness. The path of the enlightened is growing, and the path of petty people is waning and about to die out. The enlightened remain concealed, awaiting the right time. Have a truthful intent. Caution and preparedness are necessary. There still is a dangerous path ahead. Do not go on the attack. It is beneficial to go somewhere. It is necessary first to govern yourself.

Kuai: Lake over Heaven

Parting

The manager separates from mundanity.

The temporal conditioning for wine, sex, and the trappings of wealth are confusing to those who must rule their own minds.

The human mind likes these things.

A deep understanding of process, flexibility, and timing will gradually dispose of the aggregate of mundanity.

Spontaneous illumination shortly follows.

The manager should avoid excessive force.

Parting is a natural process where reason prevails over authority.

Impetuosity must give way to a path that travels between intensity and laxity.

A final warning: be alert and wary. Do not allow mundanities to catch you by surprise.

44. Kou

Removal is parting and division, meeting is coming back together and joining in association. Apply a metal brake. It bodes well to be upright. If you go anywhere, you will see misfortune. An emaciated boar leaps in earnest.

Kou: Heaven over Wind

Meeting

We have all observed the manager who is not mindful, who sits by and watches mundanity (even indulges it) and cannot prevent it.

Mundanity and obstacles are encountered constantly.

The manager who follows the path of the Tao wards them off as they are met.

The energy of the mundane is negative and acts as a brake. It stops everything and is exceedingly difficult to subdue.

One definition of arrogance would be a manager's tardiness in warding off mundanity.

45. Ts'ui

Leads to success. Culmination of a group; order. The Way must be able to unify the aspirations of people. Induce sincerity. Gather the hearts of all, unify the wills of the masses towards a common goal. Great people establish order; omit disorder and struggling confusion. Gather around what is right. Make a great sacrifice. Share the wealth, treat people generously.

Ts'ui: Lake over Earth

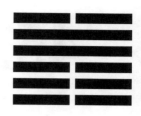

Gathering

The developmental benefit of the manager's gathering what is right is far-reaching.

This concentrates vitality and energy.

The manager who corrects others and takes correction from others can truly be described as a great person.

It is the foolish manager who watches time go by and then openly and loudly regrets a misfortunate ending.

This can also be described as carelessness in the beginning.

Since not all (or many) managers are great persons, the weak, incapable, and ordinary manager can experience joy, enlightenment, and accomplishment by borrowing the strength and wisdom of others.

46. Sheng

Rise to see great people, do not worry, progress upward. Gather, accumulate, rise. Trees grow and rise out of the earth.

Sheng: Earth over Wind

Rising

Management development can be accurately described as a climbing from lowness to highness.

It is also a meaningful goal for both the manager and his or her organization.

Rising is developmental in the extreme and is a gradual and orderly path.

Learning from those who can teach and avoiding blind practice offers the manager a clear path of accomplishment without obstacles or obstruction.

Ignorance, arbitrary action, and vain imaginings of growth result in a rising into darkness, not into illumination. It is the teacher's wisdom that restores self-realization as if it were always there.

This is a clear statement of a primary management development goal. Avoid complacency, self-satisfaction, and false joy.

47. K'un

Rise without stopping and you will become exhausted. Weakness occludes strength. Enlightened people are overshadowed and exhausted by petty people. To come through exhaustion correctly is good fortune for great people. Complain, and you will not be believed. Who will believe in you?

K'un: Lake over Water

Exhaustion

Managing is no exception to the phenomenon of exhaustion.

It is an unavoidable impasse faced continually by all individuals and organizations.

The fair-weather manager blames others and complains. His or her main concern is usually the material.

An exhausted body, however, can resolve impasse if the mind (the inner self) is not exhausted.

Accomplishment and success after hardship cannot be achieved immediately.

Gradual growth is required after exhaustion.

As in many management pitfalls and obstacles, ignorant and arbitrary actions create yet more exhaustion and are self-destructive.

A manager seeks harmonious progress.

48. Ching

You change the town, not the well. Those who come and go use the well as a well. A well is permanent. A town can even be moved. A well is never exhausted, never overflows. No loss, no gain. Quality constant. To be close to attainment is still like not having lowered the rope into the well. Breaking the bucket is unfortunate. Know the function for everything, use it.

Ching: Water over Wind

The Well

Every manager is deeply involved in the development of others such as subordinates, associates, and even superiors.

It should be simply said, however, that the most important development project for the manager is self-development.

This is a precondition to the development of others.

To attempt the development of others before attaining one's own goals will always result in not helping others and also losing oneself.

On the other hand, developing others through self-development nurtures others and oneself and represents real achievement for the organization.

Self-development is the true basis for an inexhaustible source of nourishment and development for all.

49. Ko

A well must be purified and renewed. Fire in the lake. Revolution means change. Water and fire stop one another. They rise and descend, burn and extinguish. Revolution will be trusted on the day of completion. Successful and beneficial if correct. Regret vanishes. Change the old. People cannot trust immediately. When complete, success. After, corruption and decadence, reform for everyone's benefit.

Ko: Lake over Fire

Riddance

Every manager must get rid of ego to move along a path of development and creativity.

Of equal importance to the manager is the riddance of personal desires from the inner self. This will eliminate obsolescent traits and transform him or her and the organization.

Riddance is the nonstriving revolution of the great person. He or she is then able to reform others and the organization.

Sincerity, selflessness, and illumined strength are to be strived for by the manager and those around.

50. Ting

Change things. Obedient following, combustion and cooking can bring about great success, but not immediately.

Ting: Fire over Wind

Refined Heating

In self-development, the manager achieves illumination and then refines this by following an initiatory process that solidifies his or her life and strength.

This process is developmental and good.

The refining process and procedure must be followed diligently. The manager cannot deviate.

Discard the old, comprehend essence and life, and anticipate peril. Spontaneous illumination will burn away acquired mundanity.

Illumination is promoted slowly, according to process, and carefully overseen.

51. Chen

The best people to direct the use of implements are the most mature and developed people. Be in charge, move upward. Have self-mastery. Stirring, bursting forth, moving progressively, cultivating, keeping the greater whole in mind. When thunder comes, there is fright, then laughter. Wariness, insecurity may follow; only those with discipline and seriousness will not lose self-control.

Chen: Thunder over Thunder

Action

The essence and expression of management is action.

More clearly, it is continuous action within which the manager pursues his or her own development.

In the midst of constantly repeated action, the inner activity of inward thoughts establishes the quality of the outer activity called worldly affairs.

The manager follows the path of the Tao...of inner clarity and consistency of thought...nurtures energy and contributes genuine activity with no impediment to action.

In weakness, borrow the strength of others. Be wary, especially of your own weaknesses.

The path of action of the Tao is unaffected by ups and downs.

52. Ken

Stillness connotes stability, heaviness, solidity. Stopping peacefully. Resting in the appropriate place. People are restless, moved by desire. Stop at what is unseen and there are no desires. Calm. Forget yourself. Do not get mixed up in things.

Ken: Mountain over Mountain

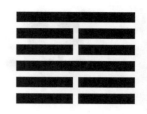

Stillness/Stopping

By stopping, the manager becomes inwardly and out-wardly still.

In this stopping, there is the stillness tested with action. This is not the stillness of inaction.

Stopping in the right place without wavering is a way to test and to learn, alternating between action and inaction.

The manager seeking the path of the Tao and the attainment of self-realization does not allow for the craving of victory and quick success.

There is no benefit from management through weakness or random speech.

Knowing the Tao is knowing when to stop.

53. Chien

Contraction and expansion. Orderly progress. No getting ahead, follow the flow. Without proper order, people overstep their bounds and violate rights. Misfortune and blame follow.

Chien: Wind over Mountain

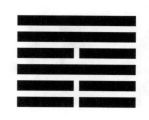

Gradual Progress

The path of the Tao leading to self-realization and attainment of goals is a subtle process...a long course of work.

Management of oneself and others toward this goal is gradual by nature.

Quick success is not the way of the Tao.

A natural and gradual progress, an orderly progress, produces the correct manner of thoroughly investigating truth and completely realizing the essence which arrives at the meaning of life.

Do not be a manager who grows old without achievement.

54. Kuei Mei

Advance and gradual progress have an objective: attaining a goal. In marrying a young woman, an expedition bodes ill. Nothing is gained. When one acts on a whim, out of place, action is not appropriate. No benefit is derived from going anywhere.

Kuei Mei: Thunder over Lake

Intercourse is Not Proper

It is improper to actively seek enjoyment in such a way that behavior obeys emotion.

The manager who follows the Tao does not use emotion to seek essence. This is incorrect and not of the appropriate time.

Use essence to seek feeling.

Manage correctly so that enjoyment comes from what can be properly enjoyed.

Be aware of those many occasions when you must await proper timing.

Manage yourself and others in such a way as to turn back from error.

55. Feng

After the gathering, growth occurs. Thunder over fire, action with clarity. Business and production boom; make sure to maintain order.

Feng: Thunder over Fire

Richness

The manager who achieves illumination and action in concert finds the path of the Tao effortless and clear.

This is the richness truly described by the words fullness and greatness. This richness is developmental.

The manager is effective in his or her thoughts and actions. Illumination and action are great. Richness has been achieved.

Seek out illumination at the beginning through the guidance of others. Strength produces richness at the beginning.

As in almost all management activities, one does not associate with the wrong people. Here we find that illumination can be blocked rather than increased.

This is a management lesson that cannot be learned too well or relearned too often.

Solitary quietude and self-satisfied rest through ignorance are empty richnesses which all managers are well advised to avoid.

56. Lu

Travel succeeds a little. Travel bodes well if correct. Go a different way after abundance ends.

Lu: Fire over Mountain

Travel

Management activity and development can be well described as a course of travel passing through without limping.

Illumination is stabilized throughout and not used carelessly. The path of management is, in a sense, a one-way trip.

The manager does not remain unduly attached to the realm(s) through which he or she passes. This is developmental. Inward disturbance and outward obscurity do not act on the manager to spoil the trip. It is not necessary here to dwell on the perils which can be brought on through weakness, lack of clarity, harshness toward others, and simple bad timing and behavior.

The manager in tune with the Tao deals with this world without destroying it and transcends this world while he or she is in it.

Enjoy your travels.

57. Sun

Wind "enters." Be adaptable. Following, docility, and obedience. It is beneficial to go somewhere and see great people. Be soft or gentle internally.

Sun: Wind over Wind

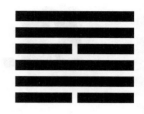

Flexibility and Obedience

It is not always possible to manage in a climate where
mutual understanding and action are unified.

Flexibility and obedience provide for endurance, gradual progress, and penetration.

This is the way of the wind. Small but developmental.

The manager is here faced with a real necessity to
apply practical steps, make gradual progress, and
continue until the great path is completed.

To follow the path of the Tao, a manager knows when
to hurry and when to relax. He or she knows what
will bring good results and knows when to stop.

58. Tui

Success. Do not use false flattery. Be gentle to those around you.

Tui: Lake over Lake

Joy

Joy is the delight found in managing along the path of the Tao.

It allows the practice of Tao. It is developmental.

The manager who finds fulfillment encounters the true reality and essence of joy.

Wealth and material gain alone are not the delight of the manager who follows the path of the Tao.

What kind of manager do you want to be?

Would you prefer to possess the joy of controlled and balanced strength or would you rather indulge yourself in self-satisfaction and outward appearances?

The Tao speaks clearly as to the correctness of joy.

59. Huan

Energy relaxes and expands, disperses and dissolves. It is beneficial to cross great rivers, be upright and steadfast. Find strength in groups of people. One must overcome danger or obstacles to remedy dispersal.

Huan: Wind over Water

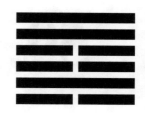

Dispersal

Dispersal means disorganization and disorder, circumstances by now familiar to all who manage.

A fundamental and critically important task for managers is always the reordering of that which is (or has become) dispersed.

Management here follows a path of progress through obedience of self-mastery and returning to appropriate order, with the manager returning to his or her original being.

Paradoxically, this is developmental.

Danger is passed by when management process and behavior follow the path of the Tao and when the manager does not lose control in situations of great difficulty and stress.

60. Chieh

*The lake is full: restrictions, discipline.
Discipline is successful, but do not persevere in
painful discipline. A sense of success results.
Balance is valuable.*

Chieh: Water over Lake

Discipline

The manager utilizes discipline to set limits that are not to be exceeded.

Every manager faces the need and challenge to practice discipline (and obedience), especially in unfavorable circumstances.

By managing along the path of the Tao, one finds peace wherever he or she is. Difficulties do not disturb the minds of those who practice reality and delight in the Tao.

Be aware that, even though discipline is developmental, failure to adapt to change and clinging to one discipline brings on danger.

We all strive for consistency of movement and adaptability to events. Discipline according to time is an important management goal. Focus also on the potential and value of peaceful and spontaneous discipline.

A last word: Do not use the strength of discipline to court danger in the hope of good luck.

133

61. Chung Fu

When you are sincere, people trust you. Those above will protect you and those below will follow. Sincerity in the center is auspicious for pigs and fish. It is beneficial to cross great rivers. Be steadfast and correct. Pigs are excitable, fish are not intelligent. Pigs and fish stand for people who are insensitive. Preserve sincerity and faithfulness.

Chung Fu: Wind over Lake

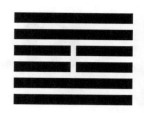

Faithfulness

Faithfulness is truthfulness from within.

This is managing with a balance of inner joy and outer accord.

By being unfaithful to the Tao, the manager risks insubstantial and inadequate power leading to failure in completing tasks.

To practice the Tao only when all is well is to follow the path of mediocrity.

It is beneficial to bear up to great obstacles and situations of difficulty and stress.

It is faithfulness to the Tao and correct practice that enable one who manages to perfect essence and life and to complete the beginning and the end.

This is the meaning of effectiveness and a job well done.

62. Hsiao Kuo

After going too far, one can succeed. Proper timing is essential.

Hsiao Kuo: Thunder over Mountain

Predominance of the Small

Predominance of the small serves to nurture the great.

To manage this developmental process, subtlety and tranquility must be maintained.

In small matters and affairs, the manager adopts a non-striving mode.

This is a matter of management versatility, since striving for the great while unable to deal with the small endangers the great.

The capability for change of pace is an essential management skill.

As a point of guidance, do not dwell too long on the predominance of the small-it is a passing mode, and excess and/or insufficiency should be avoided.

63. Chi Chi

All things are settled, success comes to the small. At first, all is well; afterward, there is disorder.

Chi Chi: Water over Fire

Settled

Illumination and danger, understanding and difficulty offset each other. This is called settlement.

To achieve this state, the manager forestalls danger, foresees peril, and completes the basis of the elixir in a stable manner.

Settlement is developmental, but arbitrary action and presumption upon illumination cause darkness to come and block the important development of settling.

Use illumination in the beginning to forestall danger. Then, even if danger exists, there is no peril.

It is always sound practice to prevent danger early on.

At the accomplishment of settlement, dismiss intellectualism and guard against danger.

Timing and balance here result in the comprehension of both essence and life.

64. Wei Chi

Things cannot come to an end. They never stop changing. Ongoing production and creation. A young fox, crossing boldly, gets its tail wet. Nothing is gained. Extreme caution and prudence are needed.

Wei Chi: Fire over Water

Not Yet Settled

Managing oneself and others most often takes place in this condition or climate.

Settlement can be achieved when the need for it can be discerned. You must manage toward a goal of settlement. You must want it.

In managing along the path of the Tao, always investigate the truth and press to seek settlement.

III
Conclusion

III. Conclusion

The Tao of Management

This work was conceived to present the teachings of the I Ching as a practical, real-life guide to management problems and opportunities. In pursuing that goal, much of the mysticism, rich imagery, and metaphor of the source material was excluded. The interested reader is urged to further explore the I Ching. Contemporary translations of several versions are readily available. This "Book of Changes" dates back almost 5,000 years and is distinguished among the great literature of the world by its secular orientation. It never dealt with religious or political teachings, but rather with quality of life and attainment of self-actualization for the individual living an ordinary life in his or her own real world.

The wisdom of the I Ching was intended to be of practical use. Its useful and beneficial wisdom and insight for all readers is evidenced by its survival in a still-living form over thousands of years. The path of the Tao is an elusive, endless, and enriching journey. It is hoped that the serious management professional reading this book has been left with useful insights into the inner self and his or her world, as well as some pressing questions having to do with relationships, work, and goals.

Be aware that questions are more important than answers and that effort, wisdom, and the quality of trying are what propels a manager and his or her organization to meaningful levels of success and accomplishment. The Tao cautions against quick fixes. The reader should certainly not look upon the Tao as a quick fix to solve real or imagined problems or to achieve what might wrongly be perceived as material or worldly success.

In managing oneself toward success and self-actualization, some guidelines from the Tao deserve extra reflection and consideration. They are:

1) Difficulty and trouble in work and personal activity do not make you different...or even unique.
2) Management is a skill process which can, and must, be learned. You can teach yourself, learn from others, or do both.
3) Management is always, to the largest extent, result- and/or task-oriented.
4) A manager must develop a comfortable, effective, and durable style of both behavior and action.
5) Self-knowledge and real awareness of oneself and surroundings are the foundations upon which a manager builds his or her repertoire of skills.
6) Simplicity and clarity of form and function are to be strived for and valued.

Bibliography

The following bibliography should be explored first-hand by the reader who has found value in this book. The wisdom and metaphor of these excellent Te Ching translations and John Heider's able "New Age" adaptation of Lao Tsu have made this writing an inspirational experience for me.

In order for this book to be relevant for the serious professional manager, much poetry and mysticism of the Te Ching was omitted from the language of this work. There is no way for me at this time to convey the pleasure, enjoyment, and true learning and enlightenment that the reader can achieve. Do not miss this opportunity to continue your journey along the path of the Tao.

Bynner, Witter. The Way of Life According to Lao Tzu. New York, New York: Capricorn Books, 1962.
Cleary, Thomas. The Taoist I Ching. Boston, Massachusetts: Shambala Publications, 1986.
Feng, Gia-fu, and English, Jane. Tao Te Ching. New York: Alfred A. Knopf, 1972.
Heider, John. The Tao of Leadership. Atlanta, Georgia: Humanics New Age, 1985.
Medhurst, C. Spurgeon. The Tao-Teh-King. Wheaton, Illinois: A Quest Book, The Theosophical Publishing House, 1972.
Schmidt, K.O. Tao Te Ching: Lao Tse's Book of Life. Lakemont, Georgia: CSA Press, 1975.
Waley, Arthur. The Way and its Power. New York: Grove Press, 1958.
Watts, Alan and Juang, Al Chung-liang. Tao the Watercourse Way. New York: Pantheon Books, 1975.
Wilhelm, Richard. I Ching or Book of Changes. Translated by Cary Baynes. Princeton, New Jersey: Princeton University Press, 1967.

Related Books Also Published by Humanics Limited

Dalton, Jerry O. The Tao Te Ching: Backward Down the Path. Atlanta: Humanics Limited, 1994.

Grigg, Ray. The Tao of Being. Atlanta: Humanics Limited, 1989.

Grigg, Ray. The Tao of Relationships. Atlanta: Humanics Limited, 1988.

Grigg, Ray. The Tao of Sailing. Atlanta: Humanics Limited, 1990.

McGregor, Jim. The Tao of Recovery. Atlanta: Humanics Limited, 1995.

Metz, Pamela. The Tao of Learning. Atlanta: Humanics Limited, 1994.

Metz, Pamela and Jacqueline Tobin. The Tao of Women. Atlanta: Humanics Limited, 1995.

Biography

The author's studies of the Taoist and Confucian culture which influences much of Asia from from Burma to Japan and beyond, began with graduate school and continued thourgh seven Years of Central Intelligence Agency assigments in the Region. Since 1958, Doctor Sadler has traveled extensively in the region both as an intelligence officer and as a private citizen. A portion of the book is inspired from Messing's The Tao of Management, published by Humanics, Ltd in 1989. Of his book, Messing wrote, "This book has resulted from a conviction on my part that much useful, practical, and even badly needed education is and has been readily available from the accumulated wisdom of our forebears." Dr. Sadler is currently writing a book relating the apparent randomness of the I Ching's binary Yin and Yang to modern scientific theory.